Along the Beach

Mike Jackson

Illustrated by

Kareen Taylerson

Evans

4

The sand at the top of the beach is
dry because the sea does not reach it.

Why is there a line of stones and seaweed along the sand?

The high tide mark shows us how far the sea comes up the beach.

They are the shells of small sea animals.

When the animal inside the shell dies, the empty shell gets washed up on to the beach by the waves.

9

There's some rubbish here, too.

10

Rubbish that is dumped in the sea
is washed up on to the beach by
the waves.

The wooden walls are called groynes.
They stop the sand from being pushed
along the beach by the wind and
the waves.

A red flag tells us that it is not safe to go swimming.

When it is safe to swim in the sea the life-guard puts up a green flag. When it is dangerous he puts up a red flag.

15

I can see some fish in these boxes.

Fishermen moor their boats inside the harbour. The harbour wall protects the boats inside from big waves.

The lobster fisherman puts some bait inside the pot and then lowers it into deep water. The lobster can climb in to eat the bait but it cannot get out again.

19

The tide goes in and out twice each day. When the tide comes in it is called high tide. When the tide goes out it is called low tide.

Seagulls search among the rock pools
for crabs and shrimps to eat.

23

Rocks and glass are worn
smooth by the movement
of the waves making
them rub against the
pebbles and sand.

25

The flashing light in the lighthouse
warns ships at sea about dangerous
rocks and sand banks.

The tide covers the sand twice a day bringing in new shells and pebbles. Each day on the beach there will be different things to find.

29

Here are some of the things that we saw on the beach. How many of them can you name? The answers are printed below, but don't peep until you've tried yourself.